A Reading First Approach

Aesop's Fables Updated

**14 New Versions of Time-Honored Fables
Partnered with the Researched Principles of Reading First**

by
Kathryn Wheeler

illustrated by
Julie Anderson

Publisher
Key Education Publishing Company LLC
Minneapolis, Minnesota

CONGRATULATIONS ON YOUR PURCHASE OF A KEY EDUCATION PRODUCT!

The editors at Key Education are former teachers who bring experience, enthusiasm, and quality to each and every product. Thousands of teachers have looked to the staff at Key Education for new and innovative resources to make their work more enjoyable and rewarding. Key Education is committed to developing and publishing educational materials that will assist teachers in building a strong and developmentally appropriate curriculum for young children.

PLAN FOR GREAT TEACHING EXPERIENCES WHEN YOU USE EDUCATIONAL MATERIALS FROM KEY EDUCATION PUBLISHING COMPANY, LLC

Credits
Author: Kathryn Wheeler
Publisher: Sherrill B. Flora
Creative Director: Annette Hollister-Papp
Cover Art: JJ Rudisill
Inside Illustrations: Julie Anderson
Editor: George C. Flora
Production: Key Education Staff

Key Education welcomes manuscripts and product ideas from teachers.
For a copy of our submission guidelines, please send a self-addressed, stamped envelope to:

Key Education Publishing Company, LLC
Acquisitions Department
9601 Newton Avenue South
Minneapolis, Minnesota 55431

About the Author

Kathryn Wheeler has worked as a teacher, an educational consultant, and an editor in educational publishing. She has published workbooks, stories, and magazine articles for children. Kate was awarded a Michigan Council for the Arts grant for fiction. She has a B.A. degree in English from Hope College. Kate lives in Michigan with her husband, Don.

Standard Book Number: 1-933052-47-3
A Reading First Approach – Aesop's Fables Updated
Copyright © 2007 by Key Education Publishing Company, LLC
Minneapolis, Minnesota 55431

Table of Contents

Aesop and Reading First: A Great Partnership

The building blocks of Reading First provide a solid foundation for a lifetime of reading. These principles are scientifically based and researched to help students take their first steps into reading that goes beyond labored word recognition into the magic of language and storytelling.

The Reading First principles are:
1. **Phonemic Awareness:** the ability of students to hear, identify, and manipulate individual sounds in spoken language.
2. **Phonics:** the relationship between letters of the alphabet and phonemes.
3. **Fluency:** the ability to read text with accuracy and confidence.
4. **Vocabulary:** the ability to learn new words and then recognize them within text.
5. **Text Comprehension:** the ability to extract meaning from what has been read.

How can you best practice these principles in order to put that foundation in place for your classroom of beginning readers? One way is to use these principles in tandem with engaging stories that will allow students to look forward to reading.

Aesop's fables are stories that have had an appeal to children for centuries. We don't know very much about the historic Aesop, but we can gather that he was a tactful person with a good sense of humor. His tact is displayed through his use of animal characters, who teach the lessons embedded in the story without offending human listeners. His humor is evident in the many complicated situations in which his characters find themselves.

In *Aesop's Fables Updated*, these familiar and well-loved stories are re-told specifically with Reading First principles in mind. Groups of phonemes are introduced in each story and identified in the warm-up exercises. Funny dialogue and repeated thoughts allow students to gain fluency through expression and repetition. New vocabulary is introduced in each story and is then used again in subsequent stories. Question worksheets allow students to apply these principles and to show that they understand what they have read. All of these details will help you teach more easily with Reading First principles.

Repeated reading is one of the methods encouraged in the Reading First program. In this book, you'll find exercises which encourage teachers to model reading of selections to students. You will also find suggestions for peer reading, including the Peer Reading Rubric on page 6 that will help your students encourage each other to gain comprehension and fluency as they read in pairs.

A natural connection to the Aesop fables is character education. On the teacher page for each story you will find the original moral of the story. These fables create a natural springboard for talking about positive traits like caring for others, thinking before you act, liking yourself the way that you are, and being truthful.

Enjoy these new versions of time-honored fables as you guide your students through decoding, understanding, and savoring the world of reading!

Peer Reading Rubric

My name is: _____

My reading partner is: _____

Here is how my reading partner did: *(Circle the right face for each point)*

Read in a clear voice.	☺	😐	☹
Sounded out words to say them right.	☺	😐	☹
Read with feeling.	☺	😐	☹
Did not read too fast.	☺	😐	☹
Did not read too slowly.	☺	😐	☹
Had fun reading!	☺	😐	☹

– Teacher's Page –
Baby Mouse Sees the World

Warm-Up Activity: Phonemic Awareness and Phonics Instruction

Introduce the students to some of the words in this story, and identify shared beginning sounds at the same time. Say each pair of words out loud and ask the class if the words share the same beginning sound or not. Encourage students to voice each beginning sound before saying "yes" or "no."

Here are some word pairs to start the exercise:

baby/big	new/meow	scream/scared
leave/little	dove/tail	monster/mouse
eat/eek	beak/pink	

If you would like to add a phonological awareness exercise to follow up, ask the students to make oral rhymes using words from the story. The words do not have to share word families for this oral exercise. Encourage the students to pair words that make sense together: nice mice; eek squeak, bright white, etc.

Background

This story is based on the Aesop fable "The Cat, the Rooster, and the Mouse." The original moral of this story is "Appearances can be deceiving."

Warm-up Activity: Fluency

Model fluent reading for your students by selecting portions of the text to read out loud. To model a rhyming section, use the Baby Mouse song from the story. Ask the students, "did you hear how I grouped the words 'give a shout?' That is because that is a whole thought that belongs together. Then I paused before I read, 'I am out'." Point out to your students that your voice got louder when you read, 'I am out.' Explain that is how you show that Baby Mouse was excited about going outside.

To help further with fluency, write the Baby Mouse lyrics on the board. Then have the students sing them to the tune of "Jack and Jill." The song rhythm will help students group the words correctly.

Peer reading will also strengthen fluency. Hand out copies of the Peer Reading Rubric on page 6 and pair students to read the story together.

Warm-up Activity: Vocabulary

Before reading the story, review these vocabulary words with your students:

bragged	gleamed	squeaky
striped	toward	monster
rooster	judge	

The story questions on page 10 contain activities about word families, multi-meaning words, and text comprehension.

Character Education Connection:

Discuss the moral of the story.
- Have you ever seen a pet that you thought would be scary, but was nice instead?
- Have you ever thought that someone would be nice or not because of the way he or she looked, or because of the clothes he or she had on?
- Why is it best not to judge people, places or things from the way they look? Give examples.

Arts Connection:

Do a play version of the story. In addition to the speaking parts, have the other students play barnyard animals or create sound effects. Design costumes and use your whiteboard or blackboard to draw a backdrop!

Baby Mouse Sees the World

Baby Mouse said to his mother, "I am *too* old enough!"

Mother Mouse shook her head. "I know that you want to leave our mouse house, Baby Mouse. I know that you want to see the world outside. But it is safe in here. The world outside can be scary."

"I won't be scared!" bragged Baby Mouse. "I am big and strong. And I can run fast."

Mother Mouse smiled. "You are not really very big," she said. "But it is true that you can run fast. All right. You can go outside for a short time. But if you see something that scares you, RUN!"

Baby Mouse smiled. His black eyes gleamed. He stuck his small pink nose out of the mouse hole. Then he dove outside. He sang a song in his squeaky little voice as he hopped along:

**"Give a shout!
I am OUT!
I am out in the world!
I won't run…
I'll just have fun!
I'll have fun in the world!"**

Baby Mouse ran into the farm yard. The sun was bright. The fence was white. He saw a big animal sitting in the sun by the fence.

"Oh, look!" said Baby Mouse. "She is so pretty. She has soft fur. She has green eyes. I have never seen anyone with green eyes."

The big animal looked up. She saw Baby Mouse staring at her. She started to wave her long, striped tail. "Meow," she said.

Baby Mouse was happy. This animal waved at him. She wanted to be his friend. "Squeak!" he said as he walked toward her. Then something made him stop.

Baby Mouse heard the flap of wings. Then an ugly monster landed between Baby Mouse and his new friend.

Baby Mouse was scared. The monster wore a red crown on his head. He had scary feet with big claws. And he had a big, yellow beak! The monster opened his beak. "EEK!" cried Baby Mouse. "The monster wants to eat me!" He tried to move, but he was too scared.

Then the monster started to scream. "COCK-A-DOODLE-DOO!" screamed the monster.

Poor Baby Mouse was shaking all over. He wondered if his new friend was scared, too. But he couldn't see her. The monster stood between them. So Baby Mouse started to run.

Baby Mouse ran hard. He ran out of the yard. He ran under the white fence. He ran to the mouse hole. He ran inside. He was safe! He was back in the warm little mouse house. "How was the world?" asked Mother Mouse.

"At first, it was fun," gasped Baby Mouse. "I met a new friend. She waved her striped tail at me. She said 'hello.' It sounded like this, 'MEOW'."

Mother Mouse asked, "What happened next?"

"An ugly monster flew out of the sky. He was scary! He had a big, yellow beak. He screamed at me. He said, 'COCK-A-DOODLE-DOO!' That means, 'I am going to eat a baby mouse!' So I ran away."

Mother Mouse smiled. "You had a big day," she said. "But you are wrong. The pretty animal you saw first is called a cat. She was the one who was going to eat you. The ugly monster you saw is called a rooster. He saved you. He flew down to scare the cat. The rooster does not eat baby mice. He is nice. He only eats seeds."

"Really?" asked Baby Mouse. Mother Mouse nodded. "The next time you go into the world, you need to think about this. You can't judge others by the way that they look."

Baby Mouse Sees the World: Questions

1. Circle the names of the Mouse family in the story.

   Mother Mouse   Fred Mouse

   Baby Mouse

2. Circle the animals that Baby Mouse saw outside.

3. Write down words from the story that belong to these two word families.

   -ouse   **-un**

   _____   _____

   _____   _____

4. Write down the two reasons why Baby Mouse says he will not get scared.

   _____

   _____

5. Write down two words from the story that rhyme with **EEK!**

   These words are not spelled the same as eek. Say the words out loud to see if they rhyme.

   _____   _____

6. Read this sentence from the story: **Then he dove outside.**

   Circle the right meaning of the word **dove** in this sentence.

   a. jump quickly

   b. a white bird

7. Read this sentence from the story: **She started to wave her long, striped tail.**

   Circle the right meaning of the word **tail** in this sentence.

   a. a story

   b. a part of an animal's body

– Teacher's Page –
The Donkey Changes Jobs

Background
This story is based on the Aesop fable "The Donkey and the Lapdog." The original moral of this story is "It is better to be satisfied with one's lot than to long for something for which one is not fitted."

Warm-Up Activity: Phonemic Awareness
Introduce the students to some of the words in this story. Ask, "Which words share the same beginning sound? Which words share the same ending sound?" Say each pair of words out loud. Encourage students to voice each beginning or ending sound before saying "yes" or "no."

Here are some word pairs to start the exercise:

farmer/fence	work/bark
good/wood	donkey/dog
Pal/pull	show/go
market/mouse	thought/goat

Then work with the words individually and try phonemic segmentation. Ask students to identify how many sounds are in each word: d/o/g.

Warm-up Activity: Fluency
This is a great story for peer reading. Students can share the story by reading the story back and forth by paragraph, or by reading "parts." For example, in the first portion of the story, one student can be the Donkey and the other student can read the part of the Goat.

Model reading that part of the story where the Donkey goes into the farmhouse. You can use great dramatic flair in modeling how to read the "sound effect" words, such as "BANG BANG BANG," "CRASH," and "EEK!" Students love to make noises like these while reading. Encourage them to read dramatically.

Hand out copies of the Peer Reading Rubric on page 6 before you pair students to read the story together.

Warm-up Activity: Vocabulary
Before reading the story, review these vocabulary words with your students:

complained	brushes	market	circles
grain	knocked	surprised	crazy

The story questions on page 14 contain activities about text comprehension, word families, and definitions of words.

Character Education Connection:
Discuss the moral of the story. A simple rewording of the moral might be, "A good job for one person might not be a good job for someone else."

- What things are you good at doing?
- Do you have a friend who is good at something you are not?
- Do people have to be good at everything? Why or why not?

Math Connection:
Create simple word problems by using the situations in "The Donkey Changes Jobs." For example, "The market is four miles from the farm. How far will the Donkey have to pull the cart to get food to the market and then back home again?"

The Donkey Changes Jobs

"All day long, it's work, work, work!" Donkey complained. "But you have a good life," said Donkey's friend Goat. "Look at your big, warm room in the barn. You have all the food you want and the farmer brushes you every day."

"Every day, I have jobs to do," Donkey pointed out. "I have to pull carts full of wood. I have to take food to the market to sell. I think I need a new job!"

"What job do you want?" asked Goat.

Donkey thought and thought. "I know!" he cried. "I want Pal's job." Pal was the farmer's dog. Pal rode in the cart that Donkey pulled. The farmer carried Pal in his arms. Every night, Pal got to eat with the farmer. Then he slept on the farmer's lap in front of the fire.

Goat said, "You want to be a dog?"

Donkey nodded. "Yes," he said. "That's the job for me!"

The next day, Donkey had to pull the cart to the fence. The farmer was fixing the fence. His tools were in the cart.

While Donkey worked, Pal played in the field. He ran in circles. He barked. He chased a rabbit. He chased his tail! "Look at that silly dog," said Donkey. "I need to learn how to act just like him." Donkey watched Pal closely.

Then Donkey pulled the cart back to the barn. The farmer sat down to rest. Pal ran up and jumped into the farmer's lap. "Good dog!" said the farmer. He petted Pal. Donkey watched Pal closely. "I need to learn how to do that," Donkey said.

That night the farmer brushed Donkey. He gave Donkey some sweet hay and grain to eat. After the farmer left, Donkey said, "Here is my chance!" He pushed open the barn door. He trotted out into the yard. Then he went up the steps to the farmer's house.

The door was closed. "How do I get in?" Donkey asked himself. He thought. He remembered the time he watched a guest come to the house. The guest had knocked on the door. "I can do that!" said Donkey. He used his hoof. BANG BANG BANG went his hoof on the door.

The farmer's wife opened the door. "Why, it is the donkey!" she said, surprised. Donkey pushed past her. He went into the kitchen. The farmer was sitting by the fire. Pal was in his lap.

"Now I will show the farmer that I am a better dog than Pal!" said Donkey.

Donkey started to run in a circle. As he ran, he knocked over the kitchen table. CRASH went the table. Then Donkey chased a little mouse that was near the fire. "EEK!" screamed the mouse. Donkey knocked over a stack of dishes. SMASH went the dishes. Then Donkey tried to bark. "HEE-HAW-WOOF!" barked Donkey.

"Now I will jump into the farmer's lap!" said Donkey happily. He started to jump.

"HELP!" yelled the farmer. "The donkey has gone crazy!"

The farmer's wife grabbed her broom. She waved the broom in front of the Donkey. "Go away!" she yelled. "Go back outside!" She chased Donkey out of the house.

Donkey walked slowly back to the barn. He pushed open the door. He lay down on his soft bed of straw.

"Well?" asked Goat. "How did it go? Do you have a new job?"

Donkey ate some sweet grain. Then he said, "I am not sure that being a dog is the right job for me. Maybe I had better keep being a donkey. At least I know how to do that!"

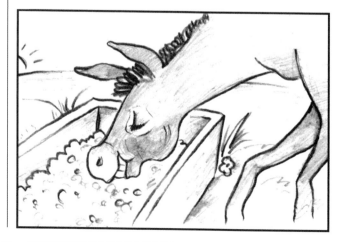

The Donkey Changes Jobs: Questions

1. Circle the name of the farmer's dog in the story.

   Goat   Pet   Donkey   Pal

2. Circle two things that Pal did in the field.

   a. jumped over the fence
   b. chased a mouse
   c. ran in circles
   d. chased his tail

3. Think of two words that rhyme with each of these words from the story.

   lap   **hoof**

   _____   _____

   _____   _____

4. Write down a reason why Donkey wants a new job.

   _____

   _____

5. Write down two words from the story that share this word family: **-ash**

   _____   _____

6. Read this sentence from the story: **"All day long, it's work, work, work!" Donkey complained.**

   Circle the word that means the same as **complained**.

   a. grabbed
   b. griped
   c. tried

7. Read this sentence from the story: **Donkey ate some sweet grain.**

   Circle which one of these is a **grain**.

   a. carrots
   b. milk
   c. oats

– Teacher's Page –
A Well of Trouble

Background

This story is based on the Aesop fable "The Fox and the Goat." The original moral of this story is "Do not trust the advice of someone in trouble." This is also the fable from which comes the famous advice, "Look before you leap."

Warm-Up Activity: Phonemic Awareness and Phonics Instruction

Introduce the students to some of the multi-syllable words in this story, and ask the students to clap their hands along with the syllables. Here are some words to start:

Tricky	Speedy	darted	answered
water	going	farmer	scrambled
silly	finally		

Then use the same words and ask the students to say the first part of the word, and then the last part. For example, for "water," the first part of the word is /w/ and the last part is /-er/.

Add a phonics exercise for this story. There are a number of words in "A Well of Trouble" that start with blends and digraphs. Introduce these to your students. Some words from the story that you might want to use for this exercise are:

Greta	thought	drank	flew
bleat	thirsty	show	chewed
close	smiled		

Say each word out loud and ask the students to identify the two sounds that make up the blend or digraph.

Warm-up Activity: Fluency

Repeated readings of the same portion of text can be a big help to fluency. Choose a short section of dialogue, such as the opening exchange between Speedy and Tricky. Ask pairs of students to give a dramatic reading of the dialogue. Suggest that they try different inflections and voices for the lines (you will probably want to model this for them first).

Be sure to have each pair of students read the dialogue at least four times. In order for this not to become tiresome for the class, team up all of the students and then circulate around the classroom to listen to the readings of each pair. You can hand out copies of the Peer Reading Rubric on page 6 for this exercise.

Warm-up Activity: Vocabulary

Before reading the story, review these vocabulary words with your students:

sparrow	trot	darted	suddenly
shady	scrambled	bleat	finally

The story questions on page 18 contain activities about word families, blends, multi-meaning words, homophones, and text comprehension.

Character Education Connection:

Discuss the moral of the story.
- What does it mean to "look before you leap"?
- Why should Greta not have trusted Tricky?
- What friend did Greta have who she could trust?
- Who are your trusted friends?

Science Connection:

In Aesop's fables, the fox is cunning and tricky. What real-life qualities do foxes have that led Aesop to this portrayal? Have your students look up facts in books or on the Internet about the fox.

A Well of Trouble

"Hot, hot, hot!" complained Tricky Fox. He walked slowly. His feet hurt. He had spent the whole, hot day looking for water.

Speedy Sparrow darted down. "Tricky, you look tired! You look thirsty!" The little bird flew around the fox's head.

"I am looking for water," said Tricky. "Can you tell me where to find it?"

Speedy flew up to the branch of a tree before she answered. She knew that Tricky was full of tricks. He might even try to eat her if she got too close! "Keep going down that path," said Speedy. "There's a deep well at the end." Then she flew away.

"A well!" said Tricky. "What good news! I am such a lucky fox." Tricky started to trot. The sun was hot. Tricky knew that soon he would get a nice, cold drink of water from the well.

At the end of the path was the well. "Hooray!" said Tricky. He looked over the edge. "Oh, no!" said the thirsty fox. "It is too deep. I cannot reach the water." He tried to lean down into the dark, cool well. Suddenly, there was a huge SPLASH! Tricky had fallen into the well.

"HELP!" cried Tricky. "HELP! HELP! HELP!" But nobody could hear him.

Tricky took a long drink of water as he stood at the bottom of the well. He was standing in the water. After the hot sun, it felt good. But Tricky knew he was in trouble. He also knew that he had played tricks on a lot of animals. None of them would want to come close enough to help him.

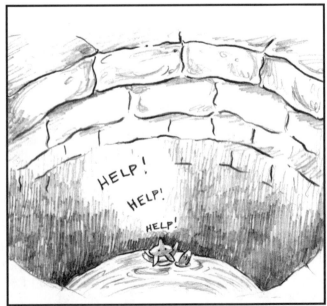

Tricky thought and thought. Then he waited. Finally, he heard a voice. It was Greta Goat. "Hello, Greta!" Tricky called.

Greta looked over the edge. "Tricky! What are you doing down there?"

"Oh," said Tricky. "It's such a hot day. This well is so cool and shady. So I jumped in. It's nice down here."

"I see." said Greta. She started to leave.

"And," Tricky called, "the water here is the best in the woods! Did you know that? I have never tasted water this sweet. Why, it almost tastes like…" Tricky thought hard, "…it almost tastes like HAY."

Greta looked down again. "Really?" she asked. "That sounds great." She looked at the water. Then she jumped down. She drank for a long time.

"This is good water!" said Greta. "I'm not sure it tastes like hay. But it sure tastes good on this hot day!" She looked up to the top of the well. "Now, how do we get out?"

Tricky smiled. "I will show you!" He jumped onto Greta's back. Then he climbed up to her head. He scrambled up her long horns. Then Tricky jumped up and climbed out of the well.

"But how do I get out?" Greta called.

"You will have to find your own way out," called Tricky. "Goodbye!" And the fox was gone.

Greta started to bleat. "Help, help!" she bleated. At last, her friend the farmer found her. "Greta! How did you get down there, you silly goat?" He ran to get help. The farmer and his helpers lifted Greta out of the well.

"I am a silly goat!" thought Greta that night. She ate her sweet hay. She chewed and thought. "But now I see two things," Greta told herself. "I will never trust that fox again. And I will always look before I leap!"

A Well of Trouble: Questions

1. Circle the name of the goat in the story.

    a. Speedy

    b. Tricky

    c. Greta

2. Who jumped into the well first?

    a. the farmer

    b. the fox

    c. the goat

3. Write down the fox's name.

_____

4. Now write down four words from the story that begin with this consonant blend: **sp**

_____   _____

_____   _____

5. Why did Greta jump into the well? Circle the correct answer.

    a. She was thirsty   b. She saw her friend the farmer.

        c. Tricky told her that the water tasted like hay.

6. Read this sentence from the story: **He tried to lean down into the dark, cool well.**

    Circle the meaning of the word **lean** in this sentence.

    a. thin

    b. bend

7. Read this sentence from the story: **"But now I see two things," Greta told herself.**

    Circle the correct meaning of the word **see** in this sentence.

    a. understand

    b. ocean

– Teacher's Page –
A Guest for Dinner

Background
This story is based on the Aesop fable "Fox and Stork." There are several versions of the moral to this story, but one version could be summed up as "Treat your guests the way that you would like to be treated."

Warm-Up Activity: Phonemic Awareness and Phonics Instruction

Introduce the students to some of the words in this story. Then work with the students to have them segment each word into its separate sounds. Example: What are the three sounds in "fox"? (f/o/x)

Here are some words to start the exercise:

had	sky	set	plan
nest	meal	like	bill

Then segment some of the words from the story and have the students say the complete word. "What word is f/o/x?"

Add a phonics exercise to finish up this game: After you have finished working with the words phonemically, say each individual word and ask the students to spell it as you write it on the board. Break the word into phonemes as you write each sound on the board.

Warm-up Activity: Fluency

Model fluent reading for your students by focusing on pauses. In this story, there are several places where dashes indicate a pause, such as, "And she is making my favorite—fish soup!" Explain to your students that these dashes are just like drawing a breath before you finish the sentence. Read them with a dramatic flair to emphasize the pauses.

There are also many questions in this story. Show the students how a question requires that you inflect your voice at the end of the sentence. Have them ask you questions and then listen to themselves as they speak. Then repeat the question back to the students, using your hand to emphasize the lifting inflection.

Peer reading will also strengthen fluency. Hand out copies of the Peer Reading Rubric on page 6 and pair the students to read the story together.

Warm-up Activity: Vocabulary

Before reading the story, review these vocabulary words with your students:

polite	foolish	trotted	favorite
stump	shallow	welcome	starving

The story questions on page 22 contain activities about word families, multi-meaning words, homophones, and text comprehension.

Character Education Connection:

Discuss the moral of the story.
- Has someone ever done something special for you that made you feel comfortable? What was it?
- Why is it important to make guests feel comfortable?
- What would the two dinners in the story have been like if each animal was thinking about the other one when they set their tables?

Language Connection:

Ask the students to make up dialogue for Tricky and Sally if they both were being good hosts to their guests. Students can try to write their words down after they brainstorm together.

A Guest for Dinner

"Sally Stork thinks she is so great!" said Tricky Fox. He had just seen the huge bird flying across the sky. "She is so polite. She is so pretty. I wish that just once she would look silly and foolish!" Suddenly, Tricky had a plan.

Sally had a nest on top of an old barn. Tricky trotted over to the barn. He called, "Sally, are you home?'

"Hello, Tricky," said Sally from the top of the barn.

"I just caught some good fish," said Tricky. "I am making my favorite meal — fish soup! Would you like to come for dinner?"

"Why, Tricky! That is very nice. I would love to come," said Sally politely.

That night, Sally flew to Tricky's den. Outside, there was a tree stump. Tricky used it for a table. He had put two shallow bowls on the stump. "Here is our soup," said Tricky. "It is all ready! Please eat."

But Sally had a problem. A stork has a long beak called a bill. Sally's bill was so long that she could not eat from the shallow little bowl. It was not deep enough. Tricky lapped up all of his soup. He thought, "Sally looks so silly! She cannot eat her soup from that bowl! She looks funny. I am enjoying this."

Out loud, Tricky said, "Sally! I am sorry you do not like my soup."

"The soup is very good," said Sally politely.

"You don't seem to be eating much of it," said Tricky.

Sally thought, "That Tricky! He is full of tricks. But I have a plan, too." Out loud, Sally said, "I think your fish soup is better than mine."

"Really?" said Tricky. "Thank you! But I am sure yours is good, too."

Sally said, "Would you like to try it? I am going fishing tomorrow. I will make fish soup. Then you can come to dinner at my house."

"I would love to come to dinner," Tricky said.

The next day, Tricky looked everywhere for food. He could not find anything to eat.

"It's OK," said Tricky. "I am going to Sally's house for dinner. And she is making my favorite — fish soup!"

That night, Tricky trotted over to the old barn. Sally was watching from the roof. "Welcome," she called. "Dinner is ready. Are you hungry?"

"I am starving!" said Tricky.

Sally had set up a table. On the table were two tall, thin vases. Steam rose out of them. "I hope you like my soup," she said. "I cooked all afternoon."

Sally leaned over one of the vases. She put her long, thin bill into the long, thin vase. She sipped some soup.

"I think it turned out well," she said. "What do you think, Tricky?"

Tricky licked around the top of the vase. He tried to push his nose down into the vace so he could get to the soup. His nose got stuck. "It smells good," he said. He pulled his nose out — POP! He licked a few drops from the top of the vase. "It tastes good, too," said the hungry fox.

Sally smiled again. "Good," she said. "I hope you enjoy it as much as I enjoyed your soup last night." Then she put her long bill into her vase and ate all of her tasty fish soup.

Tricky went home just as hungry as he had been when he came to Sally's house. But maybe he was smarter, too.

A Guest for Dinner: Questions

1. How many characters are in this story?

   one   two   three   four

2. Write down a word from the story that begins with the same blend as:

   stork _____

   Tricky _____

3. Circle the reason why Tricky asked Sally to dinner.

   a. He wanted to make a nice dinner for her.

   b. He liked her.

   c. He wanted to make her look silly.

4. Read this sentence from the story: **"Sally Stork thinks she is so great."**

   Circle the correct meaning of the word **great** in this sentence.

   a. wonderful

   b. tear in pieces

5. Circle the picture of the animal who made the first dinner.

6. Circle the word that rhymes with **stork**. Be sure to say each word out loud.

   a. stove

   b. work

   c. fork

7. Read this sentence from the story: **Steam rose out of them.**

   Circle the correct meaning of the word **rose** in this sentence.

   a. a kind of flower

   b. moved up through the air

– Teacher's Page –
King Lion

Background
This story is based on the Aesop fable "The Fox and the Lion." The original moral of this story is "Familiarity breeds contempt."

Warm-Up Activity: Phonemic Awareness and Phonics Instruction
Introduce the students to some of the words in this story, and identify shared ending sounds at the same time. Say each pair of words out loud, and ask the class if the words share the same ending sound or not. Encourage students to voice each ending sound before saying "yes" or "no."

Here are some word pairs to start the exercise:

pond/loud	hid/fast	smart/bad
path/teeth	him/again	seen/lion
bird/nod	shook/heart	

Add a phonics exercise to finish up this game: After you have finished working with the word pairs, say each individual word and ask the students to identify the onset and rime.

Warm-up Activity: Fluency
Model fluent reading for your students by selecting parts of the text with exclamation points. Show the students how an exclamation point gets the most emphasis of all marks. Ask the students, "Did you hear how I read the two lines, 'He looked at me. I think he was going to eat me!'?" That's because Tricky was more scared of the idea of being eaten than he was when the lion just looked at him.

Point out to your students that your voice got louder when you read, "going to eat me!" Explain that this is how you show that Tricky was truly scared of King Lion.

To help the students practice another section for fluency, write the words to Tricky's song on the board. Then have students sing the song to the tune of "Frère Jacques." The song rhythm will help students group the words correctly. After they have sung the text, have them read it.

Peer reading will also strengthen fluency. Hand out copies of the Peer Reading Rubric on page 6 and pair the students to read the story together.

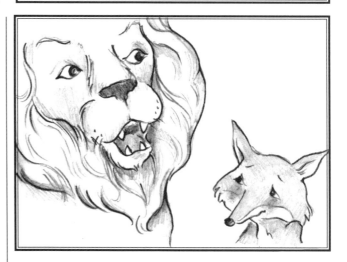

Warm-up Activity: Vocabulary
Before reading the story, review these vocabulary words with your students:

fine	beat	dare	dove
fellow	berries	hurrying	roared

The story questions on page 26 contain activities about rhymes, multi-meaning words, and text comprehension.

Character Education Connection:
Discuss the moral of the story.
- Do you have a busy street near your house? Even though it is close to home, do you still have to stop and watch for traffic?
- Even if you see a wild animal every day, might it still bite you?
- Are you as polite to people in your family as you are to strangers?

Science Connection:
Aesop was a keen observer of animal behavior. He knew that a weaker animal needs to show respect to a stronger one. Find examples of this behavior, such as when a small animal will roll up in a ball and not look directly at a bigger one. Talk about how this respect helps animals to survive.

King Lion

Tricky Fox looked at himself in the pond. "What a fine animal I am!" said Tricky. "All of the other animals fear me. They know that I am tricky and smart. Nobody is better than me!" He smiled at his own face. Then he started down the path in the woods, singing a loud song.

"Of all the animals that you see,
I know that you'll agree,
I am just the best—
better than the rest!
I love me! I love me!"

Suddenly, Tricky stopped. His heart started to beat very fast. A huge animal was standing in the path. He looked at Tricky. Then he opened his mouth to yawn. Tricky saw rows of big, sharp teeth.

"Yip! Yip! Yip!" cried Tricky. He ran off the path and into the woods. He ran as fast as he could. He did not dare look back.

"Tricky, why are you running?" somebody called from a tree. It was Speedy Sparrow.

"I just saw the biggest animal I have ever seen," Tricky said, panting. "He looked at me. I think he was going to eat me!"

"That must have been King Lion," said Speedy. "I heard he was walking through our woods. He is the king of all the animals. Even you, Tricky!"

Tricky nodded. He was still shaking. The huge lion had scared him.

A few days later, Tricky was walking through the woods again. He looked up ahead. There was King Lion! Tricky dove into the bushes. He hid there. King Lion walked past. "He did not see me," said Tricky to himself.

"But maybe it would not have been so bad if he had."

The next time Tricky saw King Lion, he did not hide. Instead, he stood at the side of the path. He bowed low. "Good day, King Lion," he said. "It's a fine day." The lion nodded and walked past.

Later that day, Tricky saw Greta Goat. "Where have you been, Tricky?" she asked.

"I was just talking with my friend, the king," bragged Tricky. "We were talking about the nice weather. King Lion said, 'Tricky, you know more about the weather than any other animal in the woods.'"

"King Lion said that?" asked Greta.

"That's right," said Tricky. "We are good friends."

A little later, Tricky saw Speedy Sparrow. "That King Lion is a fine fellow. He and I were just talking," Tricky told the little bird. "He is not scary at all."

"Really, Tricky?" asked Speedy.

"I should know," bragged Tricky. "We are best friends."

Each time Tricky saw King Lion in the woods, he would speak. The huge lion would nod and walk past.

"Why, I don't think he's a king at all," Tricky said to himself. "I should not fear him! He may be big, but he will not eat ME. After all, nobody is better than me!"

A few days later, Tricky went to pick some berries. He was hurrying down the path when he saw King Lion up ahead. "Hello there!" called Tricky. "Step aside, please. You are taking up the whole path. I am doing something very important."

King Lion looked at the fox. He opened his mouth. Then he roared. The bushes shook. The trees moved back and forth. Tricky ran for dear life.

From that day on, Tricky always bowed or hid when King Lion walked by.

King Lion: Questions

1. What is the name of the goat in the story?

   a. Speedy
   b. Greta
   c. Tricky

2. When Tricky tells King Lion to step aside, where is Tricky going?

   a. to a party
   b. to help a friend
   c. to pick berries

3. Which set of events show what happens in the **whole** story?

   a. Tricky was scared of King Lion. Then he was less scared. Then he wasn't scared at all.

   b. Tricky was not scared of King Lion. Then he was scared. Later he was not scared.

   c. Tricky was scared of King Lion. Then he was less scared. Later he was scared again.

4. Write down words from the story that rhyme with each of these words.

   start _____   rest _____

   see _____   dear _____

5. Write down one thing that Tricky tells Greta about King Lion.

   _____

   _____

6. Read this sentence from the story: **The trees moved back and forth.**

   Circle the right meaning of the word **forth** in this sentence.

   a. forward
   b. number four in line

7. Read this sentence from the story: **Tricky ran for dear life.**

   What is another way to say **ran for dear life**?

   a. ran as fast as he could
   b. ran in a life-like way

– Teacher's Page –
A Big Wish

Warm-Up Activity: Phonemic Awareness and Phonics Instruction

Introduce the students to some of the words in this story in groups of three. Say each word out loud. Then ask the class to identify which sound is the same in all three words. This is more challenging than previous exercises because the students have to listen to the whole word: **the shared sounds should not be in the same position in all three words.**

Here are some word groups to start the exercise:

nest/nice/wind (n)   oak/so/woke (long o)
still/looked/tail (l)   first/roof/follow (f)
wish/wind/away (w)1   tree/feeling/weeks (long e)
drink/stayed/dot (d)   cried/smiled/I (long i)

Add a phonics exercise to finish up this game: After you have finished working with the groups of words, write the words on the board. Which shared sounds are spelled the same? Which are not?

Background

This story is based on the Aesop fable "The Peacock," or "The Peacock's Tail." There are several versions of the moral for this story, but one is "Be careful what you wish for."

Warm-up Activity: Fluency

Select portions of the text to read out loud in a choral reading. This story has three sections that lend themselves to choral reading because of the emotional "build" from one repeated word to the next.

They are the two sections where Sidney says, **"I wish! I wish! I WISH!"** and the section where Speedy repeats **"Wow!"** to everything that Sidney says. Work on these sections first. Encourage the students to come up with a pattern of rising voices and exclamations to use for all three sections. Then have everyone read the story out loud together.

Peer reading will also strengthen fluency. Hand out copies of the Peer Reading Rubric on page 6 and pair the students to read the story together.

Warm-up Activity: Vocabulary

Before reading the story, review these vocabulary words with your students:

oak   pond   mirror   peacock
gust   proudly   towering   self

The story questions on page 30 contain activities about word families, multi-meaning words, and text comprehension.

Character Education Connection:

Discuss the moral of the story.
- Have you ever wanted something very badly, and then gotten it and were disappointed?
- What kinds of things do you wish for? Do you think your wishes will come true?
- Why wasn't Sidney happy after he became a peacock? After all, his wish came true!

Social Studies Connection:

The peacock is a symbol in a number of different cultures. The ancient Greeks talked about peacocks in their myths and plays—which is where Aesop heard of them. In medieval Europe, only the very rich could afford to own peacocks. The peacock is also the national bird of India. Make a bulletin board about peacocks.

A Big Wish

A sparrow named Sidney lived in the woods. Sidney was happy. He had a little nest high up in an oak tree. He loved to fly from one tall tree to another. He loved to sit on the roof of a house with other sparrows and look at the world. He loved the feeling of the wind in his feathers as he flew.

Then one day, Sidney went to the pond for a drink of water. It was a still day. The water was like a mirror. Sidney saw himself.

"Oh, dear!" he cried. "I am so ugly! I am gray like the dirt. I am brown like the twigs. My tail is short! My wings are small! I never knew that I looked like this!"

Sidney hid his head under his wing and cried.

For weeks he stayed away from the other sparrows. He felt too bad to go home at night to his little nest. He sat all day and all night on the trunk of a fallen tree.

Then one night, he cried, "How I wish I was beautiful! I wish I had long feathers! I wish I was a pretty color! I wish, I wish, I WISH!"

Sidney wished so hard that his wish came true. The next morning when he woke up, he felt different. He went to the pond and looked. Sidney was a peacock!

He had long feathers that trailed behind him. He could open his tail like a huge fan. He was blue and green. He shone in the sun.

"Hooray! How happy I am!" said Sidney.

Sidney went off to find his sparrow friends. The first friend he saw was Speedy Sparrow. Speedy was flying high above the woods. "Speedy!" called Sidney. "Come here!"

Speedy dove down to the ground. His beak dropped open. "Sidney, is that you?" he asked. He looked at Sidney. "Wow!"

"It is me!" said Sidney. "Look at my feathers!"

"Wow!" said Speedy.

"And look what I can do with my tail!" said Sidney. He opened his tail like a fan. He walked up and down so Speedy could see.

"WOW!" said Speedy. Sidney smiled proudly.

"You have to come with me!" said Speedy. "We need to show everybody. All the sparrows are meeting on the roof of Farmer Jones's barn. Let's go!"

Speedy took off. A gust of wind pushed him high up in the air and he sped away. Soon he was a tiny dot in the sky.

Sidney spread his big, heavy wings. He flapped them. He hopped. He tried everything he could think of but he could not follow. "Speedy, wait!" he called. But Speedy was gone.

Sidney climbed slowly up on the trunk of the fallen tree. "Here I go," he said. "This will be a good test." He hopped off the edge. But instead of sailing up into the air, he fell to the ground. He knew that he could no longer fly.

"My wings and my tail are too heavy," he thought. "I have these beautiful feathers. But what good are they if I can't fly?

Sidney thought about all the things he loved. Now he could never sit on a roof with his friends and look at the world. He could never go back to his nice little nest at night to rest. He could not fly from one towering tree to another.

Sidney climbed back onto the tree trunk. He wished as hard as he could. "I wish I was a sparrow again! I wish I was brown and gray! I wish, I wish, I WISH!"

The next morning, he hopped to the pond. His wish had come true! He was back to his old self. Sidney flew up into the sky for joy. "Hooray!" he called. "Look at me! I may be small, brown, and gray. But I can fly as fast as the wind!" Sidney knew he would never have to wish to be changed again. He was happy just the way he was.

A Big Wish: Questions

1. Circle the names of the two sparrows in the story.

   Sidney   Sally

   Speedy   Seedy

2. Circle the one thing that Sidney loved to do.

   a. go swimming
   b. fly to his nest at night
   c. sit inside a barn

3. Write down words from the story that belong to these two word families.

   -ay   **-est**

   _____   _____

   _____   _____

   _____   _____

4. **Fill in the chart.**

   Write down the words from the story that tell about the two kinds of birds.

	Sparrow	Peacock
Tail		
Colors		
Wings		

5. How did Sidney feel at the end of the story? Pick two words to tell how he felt.

   _____   _____

6. Read this sentence from the story: **It was a still day.**

   Circle the right meaning of the word **still** in this sentence.

   a. quiet and calm
   b. continuing

7. Read this sentence from the story: **He sat all day and all night on the trunk of a fallen tree.**

   Circle the right meaning of the word **trunk** in this sentence.

   a. a kind of suitcase
   b. the body of a tree

– Teacher's Page –
A Friend Indeed

Warm-Up Activity: Phonemic Awareness and Phonics Instruction

Introduce the students to some of the words in this story. Ask the students to tell you the position of a sound you select for each word. Is the selected sound at the beginning of the word, in the middle of the word, or at the end of the word?

Here are some words and sounds to start the exercise:

bright (t)	nest (short e)	bank (short a)
thin (n)	slope (p)	leaf (long e)
dove (v)	just (j)	ant (short a)
wings (w)		

Add a phonics exercise to finish up this game: After you have finished working with the words, write them on the board. Ask the students to come up and circle the selected sound in each word so the students can see the sound's position in the written word.

To finish up, ask the students to give you a rhyming word for each of the words in the list.

Warm-up Activity: Fluency

Model fluent reading for your students by selecting portions of the text to read out loud. To model a rhyming section, use Andy's poem from the end of the story. Ask the students, "did you hear how I grouped the words 'Hooray for the dove!'? That is because it is a whole thought that belongs together. Then I paused before I read, 'Out of kindness and love'." Point out to your students that your voice got louder when you read, 'Hooray for the dove!' Explain this is how you show that Andy was cheering for his new friend in that line.

To help further with fluency, write Andy's poem on the board. Then have the students do a choral reading. The poem's rhythm will help the students to group the words correctly.

Peer reading will also strengthen fluency. Hand out copies of the Peer Reading Rubric on page 6 and pair the students to read the story together.

Background

This story is based on the Aesop fable "The Ant and the Dove." The original moral of this story is "One good turn deserves another."

Warm-up Activity: Vocabulary

Before reading the story, review these vocabulary words with your students:

break	dodged	bank	clung	slope
wow!	peck	jaws	swat	breeze

The story questions on page 34 contain activities about word families, multi-meaning words, and text comprehension.

Character Education Connection:

Discuss the moral of the story.
- Name something nice you have done for a friend.
- Do you think that when you do something nice for somebody, that they would like to do something nice for you too? Why or why not?
- How does it feel when you help somebody else?

Thinking Skills Connection:

How big is an ant? Draw a life-sized picture or use a picture from a book. Then brainstorm the world as it might be for an ant. If a leaf is big enough to be a boat, what could an ant use as a table? A chair? A house?

A Friend Indeed

One bright spring day, Andy Ant headed for the pond. He had been working hard on a new nest. He had pushed sand and pulled out tiny stones. He had dug dirt. "Wow!" said Andy. "I am tired. I am thirsty, too! I need a rest. A nice, cold drink of water would make a good break."

Andy hopped to the pond. It had rained the night before. Andy had to scoot out of the way as drops of water came down from the leaves. "Watch out!" he told himself as he dodged a big drop. "Look out!" he cried as the breeze shook a branch and water rained down from it. Andy was so small that he could drown in a drop of water. He had to be very careful.

Andy was still running from all of the water when he got to the pond. And then, suddenly, Andy could not stop.

The bank of the pond was muddy and wet. Andy's thin little legs slipped out to the right and to the left. He slid down the slope to the water. Then he slid right in!

"Oh, no!" cried Andy. He tried to swim. He waved his thin little legs. "Help, somebody!"

Just as Andy was starting to slip under the water, he saw a pair of big, light gray wings over him. A voice said, "Here's a leaf. Climb on!" Andy saw the green edge of a leaf on the water. He clung to it. He pulled himself on board. The leaf was just like a boat for the little ant.

On the shore, he saw a beautiful dove. She was watching as he floated on his green-leaf boat.

"I saw you in the water," she said softly. "I pulled that leaf off a tree. I threw it into the water for you."

"Thank you!" said Andy. "That was very kind of you." His leaf boat started to float to the shore.

"You are welcome," said the dove. She started to peck at seeds that had fallen off a tree in the rain.

Andy's leaf arrived at the shore. Carefully, he stepped onto the muddy bank. Then slowly he started to climb up the slope. As he did, he saw something move in the bushes.

Andy looked harder. It was a hunter! The hunter was dressed in black clothes. He was hidden behind the leaves. He was looking at the dove. In his hand he held a net.

"He is going to try to catch my new friend!" thought Andy. "He will catch her and eat her. What can I do?"

He did not stop to think. Instead, the brave little ant ran up the muddy slope. He raced into the bushes. He found the foot of the hunter. He opened his jaws. Then he bit the hunter as hard as he could.

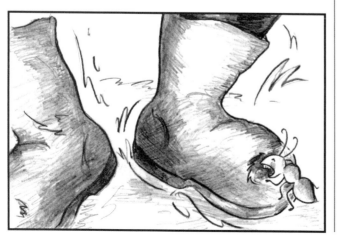

"Ouch!" cried the hunter. Before he could lean down to swat Andy, Andy ran under a leaf to hide. He looked up. The dove had heard and seen the hunter. She flew high up into a pine tree. The hunter could not reach there with his net. She was safe.

Andy headed home. He felt so good that he made up a poem about his day.

"Hooray for the dove!
Out of kindness and love,
She saved an ant,
Who hid in a plant.
And saved her right back
From a hunter in black!"

Andy hopped home, keeping away from the drops of rain. "I may be small enough to drown in a drop," Andy said out loud, "but I feel ten feet tall!"

A Friend Indeed: Questions

1. Circle the pictures of the animals in this story.

2. Circle true or false.

   a. The ant's name was Andy.

   true   false

   b. The dove's name was Doris.

   true   false

   c. The hunter wore green clothes.

   true   false

   d. The ant slipped because of the mud.

   true   false

3. Write down one word from the story that rhymes with each of the following words:

   dove _____

   ant _____

   black _____

   flew _____

4. What did it mean to feel **"ten feet tall"**? Circle the correct word.

   a. big   b. tired

   c. silly   d. proud

   Why did Andy feel ten feet tall?

   _____

   _____

5. Read this sentence from the story: **"A nice, cold drink of water would make a good break."**

   Circle the correct meaning of the word **break** in this sentence.

   a. to smash something

   b. a rest from work

6. Read this sentence from the story: **The bank of the pond was muddy and wet.**

   Circle the correct meaning of the word **bank** in this sentence.

   a. a place to keep money

   b. the edge of a body of water

The Dog and His Treat

Warm-Up Activity: Phonemic Awareness and Phonics Instruction

Introduce the students to some words from the story, and at the same time raise student awareness about middle (vowel) phonemes. Ask, "Do these two words have the same middle sound or not?" Say each pair of words out loud. Encourage students to voice the words themselves before answering "yes" or "no."

Here are some word pairs to start the exercise:

treat/set	juicy/cool	bone/honked
chased/gate	back/ran	food/good
drop/drooled	climbed/river	

For a phonics follow up, ask the students to write some of the words you have worked with on the board, and then see if they can generate word families for each one.

Background

This story is based on the Aesop fable "The Dog and the Bone." There are several versions of the moral to this story, but one version is "Only a fool is greedy."

Warm-up Activity: Fluency

Model fluent reading for your students by selecting portions of the text to read out loud. Model the section where the farm animals are calling out to Rufus.

Point out that the author has incorporated animal sounds in some of the words. Say, "Why do the geese say, 'Rufusssss' instead of 'Rufus'? What sound do geese make?" Exaggerate each animal sound and then encourage students to mimic your readings as they follow along in the text.

Peer reading will also strengthen fluency. Hand out copies of the Peer Reading Rubric on page 6 and pair the students to read the story together.

Warm-up Activity: Vocabulary

Before reading the story, review these vocabulary words with your students:

treat	perfect	juicy	drooled
honked	hissed	pasture	nerve

The story questions on page 38 contain activities about word families, multi-meaning words, an idiomatic expression, and text comprehension.

Character Education Connection:

Discuss the moral of the story.
- Have you ever wanted something that someone else had?
- Why do you think it might be better to be happy with what you have instead?
- What happened to Rufus because he was greedy?

Social Studies Connection:

Talk about a farm as a community of animals. Which animals get along? Which animals do not? What role does each animal play in the community?

The Dog and His Treat

"There you go, Rufus!" said kind Farmer Jones. He set down something in front of Rufus. He patted the dog on the head. "I wanted to give you a big treat because you have been such a good dog. Enjoy it!"

Rufus looked down at the bone. It was perfect. It was juicy. It had big chunks of meat on it. Rufus drooled. "I will spend all afternoon enjoying my treat," he said to himself. "And I will take my treat to my favorite place before I eat it!"

The dog picked up the bone and trotted off. There was a nice, cool place by the river that he liked. When he went there, he could sit in the shade. He barked at the birds. He drank nice, cold water from the river. And today, he would have a big, tasty bone to eat!

Rufus headed to the gate. A few geese honked at him, and then hissed at him. They did not like Rufus. He barked at them. He chased them for fun. Sometimes, he ate their food! **"Going ssssomewhere, Rufusssss?"** one goose hissed.

Rufus nodded. He could not answer because he was carrying his treat in his mouth.

The dog trotted out into the pasture. One cow kicked her back legs when she saw the dog. The cows did not like Rufus either. Sometimes he nipped their heels to get them to go to the barn. **"Moooove on, bad dog!"** said the cow. The dog just walked past, carrying his treat.

He trotted past the flock of sheep. They ran up a hill to get as far away from Rufus as they could. Of all the farm animals, they liked Rufus the least. It was his job to herd them from one place to another. He barked at them.

He bit them. Sometimes he took their grain to eat! **"Don't come baaaaack any time soon!"** called one sheep.

Rufus pretended not to hear. He was used to animals that did not like him. "I have my treat. I am going to chew all afternoon," the dog thought to himself. He was happy. He loved treats. He loved food of any kind.

Rufus had to cross a little bridge to get to his favorite place. As he was trotting across, he looked down at the water. There was another dog! "Hey!" thought Rufus. "That dog should not be here." Rufus growled at the dog in the water. The dog growled, too.

"Of all the nerve!" thought Rufus. Then he looked closer. "Hey!" thought Rufus. "That dog has a bone, too. But look! His bone is bigger. It has more meat on it. It is better than mine!" Rufus was mad now. He growled again. The other silly dog growled, too.

Rufus did not think very well when he was mad. And he was very mad. This dog was on his land! This dog would not run away! And this dog had a better treat! "I'll show him," thought Rufus.

"I will bark and chase him. That will make him drop his bone. Then I will have two treats to eat this afternoon!" Rufus drooled at the thought of two treats instead of one.

Rufus barked. The bone fell out of his mouth. It landed in the river with a big SPLASH. Rufus dove at the other dog. He landed in the river with a big SPLASH. But once he was in the water, the other dog was gone! Rufus did not know it, but he had been looking at himself.

"That dog took my treat!" said Rufus. "My treat is gone. How I wish I had held onto it!" Sadly, the dog climbed out of the river. He sat on a big stone. He thought about his lost bone. "Next time," the dog told himself, "I will enjoy my own treat. I won't worry about always having more."

The Dog and His Treat: Questions

1. Circle the treat that Rufus was given.

   a. a ball

   b. a piece of candy

   c. a bone

2. Write down two reasons why the geese did not like Rufus.

   _____

   _____

3. Write down words from the story that belong to these two word families.

   –eat

   _____   _____

   –ad

   _____   _____

4. Read this sentence from the story: **Rufus did not think very well when he was mad.**

   Circle the correct meaning of the word **well** in this sentence.

   a. a deep hole filled with water

   b. clearly

5. Circle the picture of the animal who liked Rufus the least.

6. Circle what was really true about the other dog that Rufus saw.

   a. The other dog had a bigger bone

   b. There was no other dog. Rufus saw himself in the water.

   c. The other dog was faster than Rufus.

7. Read this sentence from the story: **"Of all the nerve!" thought Rufus.**

   Circle the correct meaning for **of all the nerve** in this sentence.

   a. He is nervous!

   b. How dare he!

– Teacher's Page –
Jack and the Wolf

Background
This story is based on the Aesop fable "The House Dog and the Wolf." One moral for this story could be "To each his own."

Warm-Up Activity: Phonemic Awareness and Phonics Instruction

Introduce the students to some of the words in this story, and create new words out of them. Say each word out loud. Then ask the students to replace the ending phoneme to make a new word. Give them the replacement sound: "The word is back. Take away the /k/ sound and replace it with a /g/ sound. What word do you get? That's right: bag!"

Here are some words and sounds to start the exercise:

main, /l/	run, /b/	job, /t/	feet, /d/
ran, /g/	not, /d/	food, /l/	meal, /t/

Add a phonics exercise to finish up this game: After you have finished working with the pairs, say each individual word and ask students to identify the onset and rime.

Warm-up Activity: Fluency

Model fluent reading for your students by selecting portions of the text to read out loud. To model a dialogue section, use part of the talk between Jack and the Wolf.

Ask the students, "Did you hear how I dropped my voice when the text read 'said the wolf'? That's because that is not part of what they say out loud; it just tells us who is talking." Point out to your students that your voice is more expressive when you are reading the actual dialogue. Pair the students and have them practice reading just the dialogue out loud.

Peer reading will also strengthen fluency. Hand out copies of the Peer Reading Rubric on page 6 and pair students to read the story together.

Warm-up Activity: Vocabulary

Before reading the story, review these vocabulary words with your students:

collar	crunched	guard	howl
wiggled	cousin	clinked	sprang

The story questions on page 42 contain activities about word families, multi-meaning words, and text comprehension.

Character Education Connection:

Discuss the moral of the story.
- Have you ever wished you could live somebody else's life?
- What are the best parts of your own life?
- How do Jack and the Wolf each feel at the end of the story? Why?

Arts Connection:

Do a play version of "Jack and the Wolf." In addition to the speaking parts, have the other students create sound effects. For example, one group of students can be a wolf pack and howl in answer to the main-character wolf! Perform your play for a kindergarten class.

Jack and the Wolf

"You are a good dog, Jack," said Farmer Wellbeak. He patted Jack on the head. Then he put the chain on Jack's collar. "I know you will watch our house tonight." The farmer walked away. His feet crunched in the snow.

Jack watched the farmer go inside. It was Jack's main job to guard the farmhouse at night. He had his own little house, filled with hay and blankets. He went inside and laid down. His nose faced out. That way he could watch for any trouble.

Jack heard a long howl. He lifted his head. Wolves! Jack heard them a lot. "Oh, how I wish I could run free with my cousins, the wolves!" thought Jack. "Night after night, I watch the house. I have this chain to keep me here. But if the chain broke, I could live with the wolves!"

Jack thought about that. He would run anywhere he wanted. He would not have a job. He could do whatever he liked. He could howl all night long!

Instead, Jack watched the stone wall. He watched the fields. He watched the garden. Except for a few mice, he did not see anything. Jack sighed.

Suddenly, he heard a twig snap. Jack sprang to his feet! He ran to the end of his chain. His nose wiggled. A dark shape moved across the yard. It was a wolf!

"Don't bark, Cousin Dog," said the wolf. "I will not hurt you." The wolf limped up to Jack. They sniffed each other.

"Hello, Cousin Wolf," said Jack politely.

"Hello," said the wolf. "Do you...do you have anything that I could eat?

Jack looked at the wolf. He was very thin. He looked hungry. "Yes, I have this bone. It was part of my dinner. You can have it," said Jack.

He pushed the bone over to the wolf. The wolf fell on the bone. He chewed and chewed. When he was done, he said, "That was so good! Do you have food like that often?"

Jack was surprised. "Every night!" he said. "I always get a treat from dinner. But I have my own food, too."

The wolf shook his head. "That is nice," he said. "In the winter, we wolves are always hungry. There is so little food! But you are never hungry?"

"That's right," said Jack. "Farmer Wellbeak feeds me every day."

"And what do you do for this food?" asked the wolf.

Jack said, "My job is to watch at night. I bark when I see strangers. I keep the house safe." His chain clinked. The wolf looked at it.

"What is that terrible thing?" he asked.

"This is my chain," said Jack. "It keeps me from running away."

The wolf backed up. "So you cannot run free?" he asked. He sounded scared.

"No," said Jack.

The wolf shook his head. "I would rather be hungry! I could never wear a chain. I have to be free!" He ran across the field. Then he turned and called, "I am sorry for you, Cousin!" the wolf howled. In the cold air the howl sounded very loud. Jack watched the wolf run until he was out of sight.

Jack laid back down on his warm blanket. He thought about his good meals. He thought about how he slept in the warm kitchen during the day, so he could be awake at night. He thought about Farmer Wellbeak.

"I thought I wanted to be free like the wolf," said Jack. "But I am free in another way. I am never hungry. I have an important job to do. And I am loved." Jack felt very happy. He was glad he had met his cousin, the wolf.

Jack and The Wolf: Questions

1. Why did the wolf call Jack "Cousin?"

   a. because dogs and wolves are a lot alike

   b. because wolves do not have families

   c. because wolves are silly

2. What is the name of the human who takes care of Jack?

   _____

   _____

3. Write down a word from the story that rhymes with each of the following words.

   main _____   **day** _____

   right _____   **nice** _____

4. Circle the pictures of the things that the farmer gives to Jack.

5. What is the main thing that the wolf has?

   _____

6. Read this sentence from the story: **But if the chain broke I could live with the wolves.**

   Circle the right meaning of the word **broke** in this sentence.

   a. snapped in two

   b. having no money

7. Read this sentence from the story: **Jack watched the wolf run until he was out of sight.**

   Circle the right meaning of the **out of sight** in this sentence.

   a. until Jack could no longer see him

   b. until Jack could no longer hear him

Background

This story is based on the Aesop fable "The Cock and the Fox." The original moral for this story is "Liars get caught in their lies."

Warm-up Activity: Fluency

Model fluent reading for your students by selecting the paragraph that starts, "Tricky stopped." Show the students how to voice a paragraph that explains something. Ask the students, "Did you hear how my voice went up on the word 'also' when I read, 'But there were also three big dogs?' That's because it is the inflection that shows why Tricky had to be careful."

Point out to your students that your voice got louder and tenser when you read, "And then the dogs came running." Explain that is how you show that Tricky was in trouble.

Peer reading will also strengthen fluency. Hand out copies of the Peer Reading Rubric on page 6 and pair the students to read the story together.

Warm-up Activity: Vocabulary

Before reading the story, review these vocabulary words with your students:

clucked	crowed	feast	peace
lambs	greet	hen	house
porch			

The story questions on page 46 contain activities about word families, multi-meaning words, and text comprehension.

Character Education Connection:

Discuss the moral of the story.
- Why is it always better to tell the truth?
- When somebody lies, is it easy or hard to tell?
- When somebody makes up a story and pretends it is the truth, what can happen?

Math Connection:

Make up story problems that relate to "The Great Peace." Here's an example: "If Tricky had tried to steal chickens at Farmer Smith's farm twice (or two times) before, and now he is trying again, how many times has he tried all together?"

Warm-Up Activity: Phonemic Awareness and Phonics Instruction

Introduce the students to some of the words in this story, and then create new words out of them. Say each word out loud. Then ask the students to replace the beginning phoneme to make a new word. Give them the replacement sound: "The word is dinner. Take away the /d/ sound and replace it with a /w/ sound. What word do you get? That's right: winner!"

Here are some words and sounds to start the exercise:

good, /w/	fat, /h/	need, /s/	porch, /t/
told, /m/	hug, /r/	now, /c/	fox, /b/

Add a phonics exercise to finish up this game: After you have finished working with the pairs of words, ask the students to write each old and new word down. Have them underline each sound that they replaced and each new sound.

The Great Peace

"I am SO hungry!" said Tricky. He had looked for food all day. It was getting late. "I need dinner!" said Tricky. "I need something good to eat."

Tricky stopped. He was close to Farmer Smith's farm. Tricky was always careful about this farm. There were chickens and a fat rooster at the farm. But there were also three big dogs. Tricky had tried to steal chickens there before. When he tried, the chickens clucked and the rooster crowed. Then the dogs came running!

"I need to think," said Tricky to himself. "I need a good plan. Then I can catch a chicken. Maybe I can even catch that big rooster. I could have a feast tonight!"

Tricky thought and thought. Then he had an idea.

The fox ran down to the farm. He could not see any chickens, but the big rooster was sitting on the roof of the hen house.

Tricky ran to the hen house. "Hello, Rooster!" he called. "Come down here and hear the big news!"

The rooster looked down at Tricky. "Thank you. I can hear you fine from here," he said.

"Can you? Because I have very big news!" said Tricky. As he spoke, he looked around. He could see the three dogs. They were lying on the porch. They were asleep.

"Well?" asked the rooster. "What is it?"

"It's about the Great Peace!" said Tricky. He spread out his paws. "All animals are going to be friends from this day forward!"

"Really?" asked the rooster. "Who told you this?"

"Why," said Tricky, "I have just been talking with some little lambs. They are at Farmer Jones's farm. They told me all about it."

"And then did you eat them?" asked the rooster.

"No, no!" said Tricky. He held up his paws again. He tried to look honest. "The Great Peace means that we are all brothers! I will never eat another animal. Come down here. I will give you a hug!"

The rooster just looked at Tricky. "You are lying," he said.

"No!" said Tricky. "You can trust me. Trust the Great Peace."

"Well, I can try," said the rooster. He started to hop down the roof.

Tricky stood up on his hind legs. "What are you doing?" asked the rooster.

"I am standing up to greet you," said Tricky. "You are my brother now."

The rooster hopped a little closer. Tricky stretched out his paws. "What are you doing now?" asked the rooster.

"I am here to catch you, in case you fall," said Tricky. "That's what brothers do for each other!"

The rooster hopped closer. Tricky reached out to grab the rooster for his dinner. "COCK-A-DOODLE-DOO!" yelled the rooster.

Tricky looked at the porch. The three dogs had jumped up. They started running to the hen house.

Tricky started to run, too. "Why, Tricky, where are you going?" called the rooster.

"I forgot! I have to be somewhere!" Tricky cried. The dogs started to bark. They ran faster. So did Tricky.

"But aren't those dogs your brothers?" called the rooster.

"I don't think they have heard about the Great Peace yet!" yelled Tricky. Then the fox ran into the woods as fast as he could.

The Great Peace: Questions

1. Which animal makes the sound, "Cock-a-doodle-doo?"

    a. a chicken clucking

    b. a rooster crowing

    c. a dog barking

2. Why does Tricky go to Farmer Smith's house?

    _____

    _____

    _____

3. Write either **hear** or **here** to finish each sentence.

    a. We found those dogs _____ on the porch.

    b. I can _____ you talking.

    c. Did you _____ the news!

4. Circle all of the things that show that the rooster does not trust Tricky.

    a. He hops down the roof slowly.

    b. He stays on the roof at first.

    c. He wants to give Tricky a hug.

    d. He crows to call the dogs

5. Read this sentence from the story: **"The Great Peace means that we are all brothers."**

    Circle another way to say **we are all brothers** as it is used in this sentence.

    a. We have the same mother.

    b. We will all be friends now.

6. Read this sentence from the story: **They were lying on the porch.**

    Circle the meaning of the word **lying** in this sentence.

    a. stretched out on the floor or ground

    b. not telling the truth

– Teacher's Page –
A Rabbit's Life

Warm-Up Activity: Phonemic Awareness and Phonics Instruction

Introduce the students to some of the words in this story and then create new words out of them. Say each word out loud. Then ask the students to replace the middle (vowel) phoneme to make a new word. Give them the replacement sound: "The word is net. Take away the /e/ sound and replace it with a short u sound. What word do you get? That's right: nut!"

Here are some words and sounds to start the exercise:

food, short e	some, long a	dog, short i
big, short a	clover, short e	time, long a
still, short a	peek, long o	

As a phonics follow-up, point out to the students that not all words that can be changed with a vowel sound end up being spelled the same. In the list above, what happened to "peek" when it was changed to "poke?"

If you would like to add a phonological awareness exercise to follow up, ask the students to make oral rhymes using words from this exercise. Encourage the students to pair words that make sense together: big pig; still hill, etc.

Background

This story is based on the Aesop fable "The Hares and the Frogs." The original moral of this story is "There is always someone worse off than ourselves."

Warm-up Activity: Fluency

Remind your students to watch for punctuation to help them pause or stop, as well as to express the thought with the right feeling. To model the difference between a period and an exclamation point, ask the students, "How is my voice different when I read 'Run! Hide!' from when I read, 'We can go eat now'."

Ask the students to look through the text, especially the dialogue, and read questions, exclamations, and declarative sentences out loud to compare the sounds.

Peer reading will also strengthen fluency. Hand out copies of the Peer Reading Rubric on page 6 and pair the students to read the story together.

Warm-up Activity: Vocabulary

Before reading the story, review these vocabulary words with your students:

root	clover	munch	tore
peek	tease	lily pad	skip

The story questions on page 50 contain activities about word families, multi-meaning words, and text comprehension.

Character Education Connection:

Discuss the moral of the story.
- Do you think there is always someone who has a harder or easier time than you do?
- How can we help people who are less well off than we are? Give examples.

Science Connection:

When Aesop first wrote this story, he wrote it about hares, not rabbits. Read to your students about rabbits and hares. Have them compare and contrast the two animals.

A Rabbit's Life

Flora was a small, brown rabbit. She lived with her sister Dora at the edge of Farmer Smith's field.

One day, Flora and Dora went out to look for food. They had just found some tasty flowers when they heard one of the dogs barking. Dora started to shake. "Is that dog getting closer?" she asked.

"Quick, Dora!" cried Flora. "Run! Hide!" The two little rabbits ran as fast as they could. They found a place near a big oak tree and hid.

After a while, Flora peeked out from behind the root of the tree. It was quiet. "Okay," she said to Dora. "We can go eat now."

"Do you remember where those flowers were?" asked Dora.

Flora shook her head. "No," she said sadly. "I was too scared."

This happened to the little rabbits all the time.

Flora and Dora hopped out into the field. "Oh, look!" said Dora happily. "I found some clover." The two sisters started to munch on the clover. It was sweet and good.

Suddenly, they heard Farmer Smith's voice. "Quick, Flora!" cried Dora. "Run! Hide!" The rabbits tore out of the field. They jumped behind a big rock. They shook with fear. After a long time, Dora lifted up one of her big ears. "I don't hear him anymore," she said.

"Where was that clover?" asked Flora.

"I don't remember," said Dora.

"Let's go to the pond," said Flora. She was sad. Clover was her favorite meal. She really wanted some more.

As the two sisters hopped to the pond, they talked about their problem. "I think it is because of our ears," said Flora. "I can hear everything."

"Me, too," said Dora. "Last night, I could hear Farmer Smith putting the cat outside. That cat scares me."

"I could hear the mice tease the cat!" said Flora.

"I could hear the cat's feet on the grass!" said Dora.

"Every time we hear something, we are afraid," said Flora. "We can't help it. We have to run. We have to hide."

"Nobody is more scared than we are," said Dora slowly. "I am so tired of being the one who is scared all the time."

"Me, too," said Flora.

The little rabbits came out of the woods. They hopped down the hill to the pond. Their ears moved all the time. They listened for trouble. But it was still and peaceful.

Suddenly, Flora heard a croaking voice. "Listen!" she said.

Dora stopped. "I hear it," she nodded.

The croaking little voice said, "Oh, no! It's those huge rabbits! Run! Hide!"

Flora and Dora looked at the pond. They saw a family of frogs hopping to the water. They heard splash after splash as each frog dove in the water to hide.

"Look, Flora!" said Dora. "Those frogs are scared of us!"

Flora saw a frog peek out from under a lily pad. "There's one!" she yelled. The little frog dove back into the water. The rabbits went to the pond and got a drink of water.

"I feel much better now," said Flora.

"Me, too," said Dora. "Things don't look so bad. We may be afraid of a lot of animals. But the frogs are scared of us!"

Flora and Dora started back to the farm. "Hey!" said Dora. "I think I remember where that clover is."

Flora started to skip. Life was good.

A Rabbit's Life: Questions

1. Circle the name of the rabbit in the story.

      a. Mora

      b. Lora

      c. Dora

      d. Tora

2. The rabbit's are scared of all of these EXCEPT —

      a. all animals

      b. the dog

      c. the frogs

      d. Farmer Smith

3. Circle the picture of the animal that scared the rabbits.

4. Write down words from the story that belong to these two word families.

-ad	-ill
_____	_____
_____	_____

5 Underline why the rabbits felt better after they went to the pond.

    a. They were thirsty.

    b. They found that frogs were scared of them.

    c. They liked to play by the pond.

6. Read this sentence from the story: **Flora saw a frog peek out from under a lilly pad.**

Circle the correct meaning of the word **peek** in this sentence.

    a. the top of a mountain

    b. to look quickly

7. Read this sentence from the story: **Flora started to skip.**

Circle the correct meaning of the word **skip** in this sentence.

    a. pass over something

    b. to hop and leap happliy

– Teacher's Page –
Doctor Frog

Background
This story is based on the Aesop fable "The Quack Frog." One original moral for this story is "Physician, heal thyself." An easier moral to use for your students is, "Deeds matter, not boasting."

Warm-Up Activity: Phonemic Awareness and Phonics Instruction
Use some of the words in this story to help the students learn how new words can be made by adding phonemes. Say each word out loud. Then ask students to add another phoneme to make a new word. Give them the additional sound: "The word is rink. What word do you get if you add a /d/ to the beginning? That's right: drink!"

Here are some words and sounds to start the exercise:

ask, /t/	out, /p/	hot, /s/	all, /f/
us, /b/	at, /h/	he, /s/	it, /qu/

Add a phonics exercise to finish: After you have finished creating new words, ask the students to write the new words on the board and segment them into phonemes.

Warm-up Activity: Fluency
Help your students with fluency by having them read several parts of the story more than once. They can use the dialogue to make this more fun by adding a different emphasis to a line during each reading. Tell the students, "Listen as I read this line: 'Sally said, We need a doctor.' Now listen as I read, 'We need a doctor?' and 'We need a doctor!' How is each one different?" Ask individual students to read the dialogue lines with different emphasis and then talk as a class about the meaning that each emphasis adds.

Peer reading will also strengthen fluency. Hand out copies of the Peer Reading Rubric on page 6 and pair the students to read the story together.

Warm-up Activity: Vocabulary
Before reading the story, review these vocabulary words with your students:

ow!	thorn	ill	limped
famous	den	secret	boasting

The story questions on page 54 contain activities about word families, multi-meaning words, and text comprehension.

Character Education Connection:
Discuss the moral of the story.
- Have you ever said you could do something, but you knew you could not?
- Why did the frog want the animals to think he was famous?
- Why is it best not to brag?

Language Arts Connection:
Read another book or story about boasting or bragging to the students. One possibility is the Zuni tale about a Coyote bragging to the crows who teach him how to fly. Another is the pourquoi story, "How The Chipmunk Got His Stripes."

Doctor Frog

"OW!" cried Sally Stork. "I hurt my bill on this stone."

Tricky the fox limped up to her. "I think I have a thorn in my paw," he said. "I was going to ask you to help me. Can you pull it out?"

"I cannot, now that my bill is hurt," said Sally.

Speedy Sparrow flew down from the barn roof. "Did you know that Will Wolf is not feeling well?" he said. "His nose is hot. That means he is ill."

Sally said, "We need a doctor."

"Yes!" said Tricky. "We need a doctor for all the animals in the woods."

"Speedy," said Sally, "you could go look for a doctor. You could fly over all of the woods. See if you can find somebody who can help us."

"I will!" said Speedy. He darted up into the sky.

The animals waited and waited. Sally's bill hurt so much she put her head under her wing. Tricky limped and hopped and complained. Up in his den, Will Wolf woke up. He hurt all over. The wolf watched to see if the doctor had come yet.

"Look!" called Sally. "There is Speedy!"

"At last!" said Tricky.

Will Wolf slowly came out of his den and went down to hear what Speedy had to say.

"I found a doctor," said Speedy. "He is coming soon. It might take him a while. He has to hop the whole way."

"Hop? What kind of doctor is he?" asked Sally.

"His name is Doctor Frog," said Speedy.

"I have never heard of him," said Tricky.

"He says that he is known far and wide," said Speedy.

The animals waited. Then they heard a voice. "I am here!" said the voice. "I am the famous Doctor Frog!" A frog hopped out of the woods. He wore a black hat on his head and he held a bottle.

"What is in that bottle?" asked Sally.

"This? This is a secret cure!" said Doctor Frog. "The cure in this bottle can help you if you feel bad."

"Can it take thorns out of paws?" asked Tricky.

"Of course!" said Doctor Frog.

"Can it help make Will Wolf feel better?" asked Speedy.

"Yes!" said Doctor Frog.

Sally looked at the bottle. "It looks like water from the pond," she said. Then she looked closely at Doctor Frog. "Can you use this drink to make green skin turn pink?" she asked.

"Yes!" said Doctor Frog. "It can do anything!"

"Then drink it," said Tricky. "Let's see if you turn into a pretty pink frog."

Doctor Frog blinked. "Umm...It might not work that fast," he said.

"Can you use this drink to fix eyes that stick out?" asked Sally.

"Of course!" said Doctor Frog. "My cures are famous!"

"Then drink it," said Tricky. "Let's see if it fixes your eyes."

Doctor Frog looked at the bottle. He looked at the animals. Then he backed up slowly. "I will leave you this bottle," he said. "I must be on my way." He started to hurry off. When he was far away in the woods, he shouted to other animals, "Here I come! I am the famous Doctor Frog!"

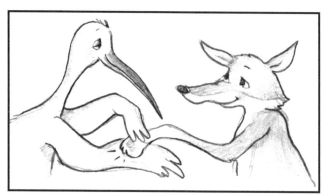

Sally laughed. "Tricky, I think I can help you pull out that thorn now," she said. "Then you can take some soup to Will Wolf. I don't think that silly boasting frog can help us. We will just have to help ourselves!"

Doctor Frog: Questions

1. Circle the name of the stork in the story.

      a. Sally

      b. Will

      c. Speedy

      d. Tricky

2. Circle another word that has the same meaning as **boasting**.

      king   b. bragging

3. Circle the pictures of the animals in this story.

...y that belong to these two word families.

-ill

   —   _____

   —   _____

5. What ... Plot Doctor Frog's bottle?

_____

6. Read this sentence from the story: "**I have never heard of him,**" said Tricky.

Circle the correct meaning of the word **heard** in this sentence.

    a. a group of cows

    b. to have been told about something

7. Read this sentence from the story: "**He has to hop the whole way.**"

Circle the correct meaning of the word **whole** in this sentence.

    a. entire

    b. a round opening

– Teacher's Page –
Mother Lark Moves

Background
This story is based on the Aesop fable "The Lark and Her Children." The original moral of this story is "If you want something done, do it yourself."

Warm-Up Activity: Phonemic Awareness and Phonics Instruction

Introduce the students to some of the words in this story, and identify shared phonemes at the same time. Say each pair of words out loud. Ask, "What sound is the same in bag and grab?" Students should answer that the ending sound, /g/, is the same in both words.

Here are some word pairs to start the exercise:

rest/right	eat/right	woods/wheat
tell/help	must/mother	come/son
men/down	flew/field	

Add a phonics exercise to finish up this game: After you have finished working with the words, write some of them on the board and develop lists of word families for them.

Warm-up Activity: Fluency

Model fluent reading for your students by selecting mirrored portions of the text to read out loud. This story is written so that the farmer's words, the baby larks' insistence that it's time to leave, and Mother Lark's replies to her babies are nearly the same each time. Read the sections as a choral reading. Show the students how to phrase each repeated line.

To help further with fluency, choose a fairy tale that has similar repetition (such as "The Three Pigs"). Have your class do a choral reading of the fairy tale.

Peer reading will also strengthen fluency. Hand out copies of the Peer Reading Rubric on page 6 and pair the students to read the story together.

Warm-up Activity: Vocabulary

Before reading the story, review these vocabulary words with your students:

wheat	enough	ripe	uncles
combed	follow	beat	settle

The story questions on page 58 contain activities about word families, multi-meaning words, and text comprehension.

Character Education Connection:
Discuss the moral of the story.
- What are the best things about being able to do something for yourself?
- Have you ever had to wait for someone to help you with something?
- What does the farmer decide at the end of the story?

Social Studies Connection:
Talk with your students about harvest time. Study some of the old traditions that happened at harvest time, such as neighbors working together in each other's fields and holding harvest feasts and dances after the work was done.

"Goodnight, little ones," said Mother Lark, tucking wheat around her babies to keep them warm. "Rest well."

"Mama, are we going to move tomorrow?" asked Lucy Lark.

"I do not know," said Mother Lark. "We need to watch and listen. Then we will know the right day to move."

Mother Lark had built her nest in the middle of a wheat field. Her little babies had been born there. The nest was on the ground.

The babies could hop out without falling. They could eat the wheat seeds that fell on the ground. But Mother Lark had told them that someday they would have to move.

"The farmer who owns this field will cut down all the wheat," she said. "It will be at the end of summer. We will move to the woods right before he cuts the wheat. We will go to live in a big tree. You will then be old enough to fly to our new home."

The next day, Farmer Jones walked out into the field. He called to his son, "Look! The wheat is ripe. Call our neighbors. Tell them to come and help us cut the wheat down. It is ready."

"Mama! Mama!" cried Lettie Lark. "We must go!"

Mother Lark smiled. "Not yet," she said. "We can enjoy all this good seed for a while longer."

The next day, Farmer Jones walked out into the field. He called to his son, "We need to cut down this wheat. Call your uncles and cousins. Ask them to come and help us cut the wheat down. It is ready."

"Mama! Mama!" cried Lindy Lark. "We must go!"

Mother Lark combed Lindy's feathers with her beak. "Not yet," she said. "We can all enjoy this nice sun and our little nest for a while longer."

That night, Lucy, Lettie, and Lindy talked. "How does Mama know that it is not yet time to move?" asked Lettie.

"Maybe she is wrong! Maybe we will get hurt when the men come to cut the wheat!" said Lindy.

"Mama knows everything," said Lucy. "Don't worry. She will know the right time to go."

The other two larks looked at Lucy. "You're the one who thinks she knows everything!" said Lettie.

"Am not!" shouted Lucy.

"ARE TOO!" shouted Lindy.

Mother Lark flew down to the nest. "Children, stop that! Settle down. Go to sleep. It is a beautiful night."

She tucked warm wheat around the little birds. They looked at the stars together. Soon the babies were asleep.

The next day, Farmer Jones walked out into the field. He called to his son, "We need to cut down this wheat. We cannot wait for others to help us. You and I will start work together."

Mother Lark flew down to the little nest in the field. "Children, it is time to move!" she said. "I have finished our new home. Now, follow me!"

Mother Lark flew up above the field. First Lucy flew after her. Then Lettie flew after Lucy. Then Lindy flew after Lettie. They beat their little wings as hard as they could. They flew after their mother to a big tree at the edge of the field. High up in the tree was a brand-new nest.

The three lark children settled into the nest. "Mama, I have a question," said Lindy Lark. "How did you know that today was really the day to move? That farmer said every day that it was time to cut the wheat."

Mother Lark smiled. "When a man is ready to do his work himself, he will get it done that very day," she said. "So today was the day to move!"

Name:

Baby Mouse Sees the World: Questions

1. What does **ripe** mean?

   a. ready to plant

   b. ready to grow

   c. ready to eat

2. What is a **lark**?

   a. a kind of bug

   b. a kind of bird

   c. a kind of cat

3. Write down words from the story that belong to these two word families.

   -ut

   _____

   _____

   -eed

   _____

   _____

4. Circle the reason why Mother Lark knew it was time to move.

   a. It was the end of the summer.

   b. The son said it was time to cut wheat.

   c. The farmer was ready to cut the wheat himself.

5. Write down the names of the baby larks.

   _____

   _____

   _____

6. Read this sentence from the story: **"I do not know," said Mother Lark.**

   Circle the meaning of the phrase **I do not know** in this sentence.

   a. I am not sure.

   b. I have not said.

7. Read this sentence from the story: **"Children, stop that! Settle down."**

   Circle the meaning of the phrase **settle down** in this sentence.

   a. Be quiet.

   b. Watch closely.

– Teacher's Page –
Betsy and Bossy

Background

This story is based on the Aesop fable "The Milkmaid and Her Pail." The original moral of this story is "Don't count your chickens before they're hatched."

Warm-Up Activity: Phonemic Awareness and Phonics Instruction

Introduce the students to some of the words in this story, and play a phoneme game at the same time. Say each of the following trio of words out loud. Ask your class, "Which one doesn't belong?" Students should recognize the word with the odd phoneme. Begin the game by telling the students to listen for either the beginning or ending sound in each word. Later you can let the students guess which sound creates the "odd word out."

Here are some word trios to start the exercise:

Beginning Sounds:

Bossy/Betsy/Greta   sighed/best/something
think/that/plant   pail/bow/pink

Ending Sounds:

milk/good/liked   right/toss/dress
will/stool/back   think/milk/smart

Add a phonics exercise to finish up this game: After you have finished working with the trios, ask the students to write the words out and identify the onset and rime.

Warm-up Activity: Fluency

Model fluent reading for your students by selecting a portion of the text to read out loud. To model a more challenging dialogue section, concentrate on the lines where Bossy "talks" to Betsy through physical actions. The line, "That meant..." appears, followed by Bossy's reply in human language.

Read some of these lines out loud to the students. Point out that the phrase "that meant" in these sentences is used very much like the word "said" in regular dialogue. Show the students how you pause after "that meant" in the same way as the pause after the word "said."

Peer reading will also strengthen fluency. Hand out copies of the Peer Reading Rubric on page 6 and pair the students to read the story together.

Warm-up Activity: Vocabulary

Before reading the story, review these vocabulary words with your students:

sighed   milked   stool   hatch
rich   trade   toss   split

The story questions on page 62 contain activities about word families, multi-meaning words, and text comprehension.

Character Education Connection:

Discuss the moral of the story.
- Have you ever counted on something happening and then it didn't? How did you feel?
- What can happen when you "count your chickens before they're hatched"?
- Is it better to want something you don't have, or to like what you do have?

Math Connection:

Do a "chickens before they're hatched" story problem! Here is an example: "If you could get two dollars for your butter and the eggs are ten cents each, how many eggs could you buy?"

Betsy and Bossy

"Milking time, Bossy!" called Betsy. Bossy sighed. She did not mind being milked, but Betsy talked and talked and talked. Bossy liked her barn. The sun came in through the windows. The hay was sweet and good. And it was nice and quiet—except at milking time.

"Good afternoon, Bossy!" said Betsy. She was carrying her pail on her head. Betsy liked to carry the pail this way. "I hope you had a good day." Bossy swished her tail. That meant, "Yes."

"That's great!" said Betsy. "Guess where I am going tonight? I'm going to the dance. All the farmers will be there. Farmer Jones will be there. And I bet his son Jeff will be there, too. Jeff thinks he is so wonderful," said Betsy. She set down the pail. She got the stool to sit on. "Just because he is good-looking! Well, I would never marry him!"

Bossy listened quietly. She knew that Betsy liked Jeff the best.

"I wish I had a new dress to wear," said Betsy as she started to milk the cow. "I would like a pink dress. Or maybe a blue one. Something with a nice, big bow in the back. What do you think?"

Bossy gave a low moo. That meant, "It sounds nice."

"I think it would be pretty, too! But Mother says we do not have enough money for a new dress right now. But who knows? Maybe we will have a good year now. We might plant some extra wheat. Then we will have more to sell when we cut it. Or maybe we could buy some eggs."

Bossy stamped her foot. That meant, "Why do you want eggs?"

"Oh, Bossy! Everybody knows that. You get the eggs to hatch. Then you have little chicks. They grow up to be chickens. They lay more eggs. Then you can sell some eggs and hatch some so you have more chickens."

Bossy nodded her head.
That meant, "I see."

"Look at this good, rich milk you just gave me, Bossy!" said Betsy. She stood up with the milking pail. "I know what I will do. I will make butter with this milk. Then I will take the butter into town. I will trade it for some eggs. Then I will raise some little chicks. Soon I'll have eggs to sell!"

Bossy listened. Betsy lifted the pail and put it on her head.

"When I sell my eggs, I will have money for my new pink dress! Or maybe a blue dress. Then I can wear the dress at the next dance! All the boys will come and ask me to dance. But if that Jeff Jones comes to ask me....why, do you know what I will do?"

Bossy shook her head. That meant, "No, I don't know."

"Why, Bossy, I would never dance with that stuck-up Jeff! I won't even say no to him. I'll just toss my head — like this!"

Bossy raised her head and flicked her ears. That meant, "Watch out!" But it was too late. When Betsy tossed her head, the pail fell down on the ground. It split in two. All of the milk ran out across the floor of the barn.

"Oh, no! My butter! My eggs! My chicks! My new dress!" cried Betsy. Then she ran from the barn.

Bossy looked at the spilled milk. She gave a low moo. Greta Goat looked over from her end of the barn. "That Betsy is a silly girl," said Greta.

"She does talk a lot," said Bossy. "And she dreams a lot, too."

"Well," said Greta, "I think it is smart not to count your chickens before they hatch!"

Betsy and Bossy: Questions

1. How many characters are in this story?

   a. one
   b. two
   c. three
   d. four

2. Circle the first thing that Betsy says she will buy in the story.

   a. dress
   b. butter
   c. eggs
   d. chickens

3. Write down words from the story that belong to these two word families.

   -arry

   _____

   _____

   -ail

   _____

   _____

4. Why does Betsy want to make some money?

   _____

5. Write down two words from the story. One word rhymes with **pink** and the other word rhymes with **blue**.

   These words are not spelled the same as the color words.
   Say each word out loud to see if it rhymes.

   _____   _____

6. Read this sentence from the story: **"Look at this good, rich milk you just gave me, Bossy!"**

   Circle the right meaning of the word **rich** in this sentence.

   a. thick and creamy

   b. having lots of money

7. Read this sentence from the story: **She set down the pail.**

   Circle the right meaning of the word **pail** in this sentence.

   a. white

   b. bucket

Answer Key

Baby Mouse Sees the World 10
1. Mother Mouse, Baby Mouse
2. cat, rooster
3. house, mouse; fun, run
4. He is big and strong; he can run fast.
5. squeak, beak
6. a. jump quickly
7. b. a part of an animal's body

The Donkey Changes Jobs 14
1. Pal
2. c. ran in circles; d. chased his tail
3. nap, flap, roof, woof
4. He is tired of working so hard; he doesn't want to do his jobs. *(Answers will vary.)*
5. crash, smash
6. b. griped
7. c. oats

A Well of Trouble 18
1. c. Greta
2. b. the fox
3. Tricky
4. spent, Speedy, sparrow, splash
5. c. Tricky told her that the water tasted like hay.
6. b. bend
7. a. understand

A Guest for Dinner 22
1. two
2. starving, tried
3. c. he wanted to make her look silly
4. a. wonderful
5. Tricky
6. c. fork
7. b. moved up through the air

King Lion 26
1. b. Greta
2. c. to pick berries
3. c. Tricky was scared of King Lion.
   Then he was less scared.
   Later he was scared again.
4. heart, best, agree, fear
5. He is a fine fellow; he is not scary; he and Tricky are best friends. *(Answers will vary.)*
6. a. forward
7. a. ran as fast as he could

A Big Wish 30
1. Sidney, Speedy
2. b. fly to his nest at night
3. day, gray, away, nest, test, rest
4.

	Sparrow	Peacock
Tail	short	long
Colors	gray and brown	green and blue
Wings	small	big and heavy

5. happy, joy
6. a. quiet and calm
7. b. the body of a tree

A Friend Indeed 34
1. ant, dove
2. a. true; b. false; c. false; d. true
3. love, plant, back, threw
4. d. proud; because he saved the dove's life *(Answers will vary.)*
5. b. a rest from work
6. b. the edge of a body of water

The Dog and His Treat 38
1. c. a bone
2. He chased them; he ate their food
3. treat, meat, eat, bad, mad
4. b. clearly
5. sheep
6. b. There was no other dog. Rufus saw himself in the water.
7. b. How dare he!

Jack and the Wolf 42
1. a. because dogs and wolves are a lot alike
2. Farmer Wellbeak
3. chain, hay, night, mice
4. food, pats on the head, a little house
5. Freedom
6. a. snapped in two
7. a. until Jack could no longer see him

The Great Peace 46
1. b. a rooster crowing
2. because he wants to eat a chicken
3. a. here; b. hear; c. hear
4. a. He hops down the roof slowly.
   b. He stays on the roof at first.
   c. He crows to call the dogs.
5. b. We will all be friends now.
6. a. stretched out on the floor or ground

Answer Key

A Rabbit's Life 50
1. c. Dora
2. c. the frogs
3. dog
4. sad, pad, bad, still, hill
5. b. They found that frogs were scared of them.
6. b. to look quickly
7. b. to hop and leap happily

Doctor Frog 54
1. a. Sally
2. b. bragging
3. frog, fox, stork, wolf
4. bill, Will, think, drink, pink
5. water from the pond *(Answers will vary.)*
6. b. to have been told about something
7. a. entire

Mother Lark Moves 58
1. c. ready to eat
2. b. a kind of bird
3. but, cut, seed, need
4. c. The farmer was ready to cut the wheat himself.
5. Lucy, Lettie, Lindy
6. a. I am not sure.
7. a. Be quiet.

Betsy and Bossy 62
1. c. three *(Betsy, Bossy, and Greta)*
2. c. eggs
3. carry, marry, pail, tail
4. so she can buy a new dress *(Answers will vary.)*
5. pink, think, blue, too, do, two, moo
6. a. thick and creamy
7. b. bucket